Why Tennis?

A Foundational Guide for Parents and Coaches

DANIEL BEZMAN

Dedicated to my parents.

Copyright © 2020

All rights reserved. No portion of the book may be reproduced or utilized in any form or by any means, electronic or mechanical, including photocopying, recording, or by any other information storage and retrieval system, without permission in writing from the author.

If you enjoyed this book and are interested to find out more about the content e-mail me at **danielbezman@gmail.com**

Table of Contents

Introduction 5

I. Systems Thinking and Mental Models 9

II. Developmental Models 15

III. Physical Literacy 25

IV. Sports Psychology 31

V. Nutrition and Hydration 39

VI. Recovery Protocols – The Key to Longevity 43

VII. Periodization and Planning 49

VIII. Sports Science 51

IX. Athlete Management 55

X. Tournaments and Ranking Systems 59

XI. Positive Player-Parent-Coach Interactions 61

Conclusion 65

References 69

Introduction

If you are reading this book, it means that you are serious about your child's development as a tennis player. You are willing to do everything you can to prepare your child for success as a tennis player. This is a noble pursuit, and if you have done some research of your own, you probably realize how much information is available on this topic.

In writing this book, I have the goals of informing people about the pitfalls into which countless families fall when it comes to tennis and of providing a more systematic framework for parents, from the perspective of a coach. This guide is intended for parents who are willing to be hands-on, to put in the hours, to sacrifice, and to be realistic about how difficult this road can be. It's for parents who genuinely want to know what it's going to take to have a shot at the top levels of the game of tennis. Why? Because the parents and the relationship they build with the coaches are among the most important factors in a child's success – or failure – in tennis and life.

That is why I have set out on a quest: to find the most efficient and effective approaches to developmental coaching possible. Over the last fifteen years, I have devoted myself to coaching tennis. This is my life. It's *everything* to me.

Briefly, I coached on the WTA Tour and in the biggest tennis academies around the world, including Mouratoglou Tennis Academy.

I have participated in some of the world's most competitive junior tennis environments. Still, my true passion is developmental coaching, focusing on building young talent from an early age.

This work can be wonderfully fulfilling, but it can be heartbreaking, too. Also, I have had my share of tough learning experiences. I have watched parents pour their hearts into their children's tennis development, only to fall *way* short. It's always frustrating to watch, and it's sort of like a perpetual pattern.

Is that to say that every case is *exactly* the same? No, of course not. Still, I have observed many of the same patterns that lead to success and failure, and these patterns have *nothing* to do with genetics. Based on these global patterns, I have concluded that one of the main reasons for these shortcomings is a lack of *fundamental knowledge* that every parent and coach should possess. Clearly, this is not a problem of having enough information. The issue is in having the *key information and applying it in an optimal way*. Unless you have equipped yourself with the *right* minimum knowledge necessary, you can make a negative, rather than a positive, impact on your kid.

I do not intend for this book to be an in-depth analysis of tennis skill education. Let me make that clear right up front. Instead, I try to focus on the underlying elements that can make tennis training more efficient. To give you a quick example: At a young age, athletes must play a variety of sports and games so that they can develop the fundamentals of athleticism. Without those fundamentals, athletes get hurt and can't keep up. Then they feel confused and disappointed because of their failure. The athletes who *do* learn the fundamentals, however, tend to excel.

But don't worry! In this guide, I have laid out the fundamental pillars that help and support the development of a successful tennis player, alongside some of the more advanced and involved concepts. Everything is organized into an easier-to-digest, process-driven format.

As a coach, I need your *help and cooperation*. When you are aware of the intricacies of this sport, you will see why it is so important to have a system in place from the beginning. This whole process could take up to fifteen years of your time, energy, and resources. When you understand why your child is working on a specific skill or strength at a specific time, you will more clearly see and understand your role in the system, which will make my job easier as the coach.

My coaching philosophy is all about progressive development based on a long-term plan, drawing on my years of experience and expertise, including the ups and downs.

With that said, I need you to be on the same page as me for any of this to work! Take it all in, see what sticks, and when you are done, you should hopefully feel more comfortable entrusting your child's success in tennis to the right team – and become more aware of what the right coach will say and do, as well as know what to demand and expect.

I am very passionate about fundamentals and learning tennis *the right way*. Is my coaching style going to fit every parent or student? Absolutely not. That is why I want to make my process clear from the beginning. If you get to the last page of this book and think *This isn't for me*, then you have just saved us both a lost decade, and I thank you.

In my experience, parents who are better informed about what goes into developing world-class athletes will become better able to fill their roles in the developmental *system*. As the parent, you are going to make an outsized impact on your child's development one way or another. Whether that impact is good or bad is up to you. If the ego gets in the way, or if you have bought into pseudoscience, you may start to go down some nasty paths: pushing your child to skip developmental stages, pressuring your child to win at too young an age, interfering in the coach's lessons. None of this leads anywhere beneficial, least of all in your child's development. The most likely outcome is that you will run your child ragged long before he or she has reached his or her full potential.

Now, don't get me wrong. I don't have a problem if you decide to be the coach. However, you should make that clear from the outset, as this will avoid confusion for everyone, especially the child. This book is not meant to turn you into a coach or an expert of any kind. Clearly, there is not enough information in here for you to troubleshoot tennis development. What this book does provide is *fundamental information* that you can use to recognize and better carry out your role in your child's development as a tennis player. This, in turn, facilitates the training process – nothing less, nothing more.

Again, this begs the question: Why tennis?

Let's answer that one together – starting with the right thinking.

I. Systems Thinking and Mental Models

"Everything is simple if you really want it to be!"

~ Vladeta Radivojevic

I do not mean to build up too much optimism or downplay the complexity of this process. However, I believe that, through proper planning, we can make anything simpler.

How? By adopting **systems thinking and mental models**.

Mental models are how we understand the world. They shape our understanding of reality, how we make connections between ideas, and which opportunities we see. When we use mental models, we are *simplifying complexity*. This is an incredible process, enabling us to put different weights to concepts and form representations of the components that work in conjunction with each other in a system. Because we could never hope to keep all of the details of the world in order in our brains, we can apply models to them, thereby dividing them into more manageable chunks.

Adopting this method, we can look at the individual parts that make up any system and figure out a better way for them to fit together. S*ystems thinking* considers the *interactions* between the parts in a system instead of thinking about them as independent of each other in any way. This enables us to start thinking in recurring, reinforcing, and balancing loops instead of straight lines, which empowers us to think from a ***preventive mindset*** rather than a reactive one.

Here is an overview of systems thinking:

Figure 1. **Iceberg model - Systems Thinking**

Next, let's turn our attention to a specific type of system of a tennis player – a microcycle.

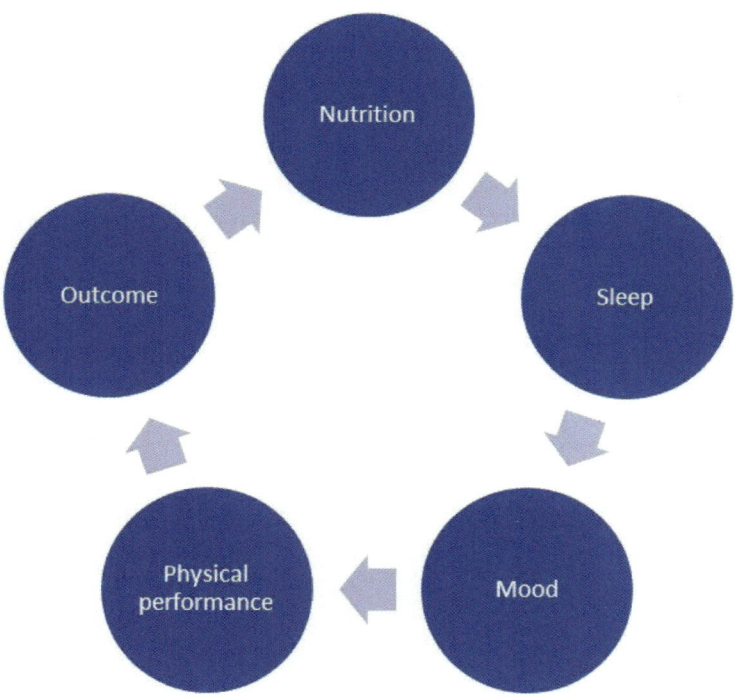

Figure 2. Microcycle sample of a tennis player

One quote that I often think about when I am talking about systems thinking is "***Managers do not solve problems, they manage messes***." This comes from Russell Ackoff, an operations theorist. As coaches and parents, we can easily create a "mess" if we ignore the interconnectedness of all the parts of trains. We can avoid this through awareness.

How does all of this apply to tennis specifically? Throughout tennis training, athletes must be responsible for other roles and duties. Within tennis, an athlete must consider nutrition, practice, and competition – all in the same season, inevitably. When the different roles and responsibilities clash with each other, one will tend to sabotage another.

When they work in alignment, however, we see that they become more than the sum of their parts, engineering momentum that would have been impossible to create when they were working alone.

Strategic planning does not happen overnight. It requires us to define a strategic objective, general operating principles, and working procedures. From *there*, we can make some progress. By trusting the correct leader in any situation, we can start to correctly shift, dissect, and analyze any system, escaping the sabotage that would otherwise occur and pinpointing the root causes of the flaws in the system. The most important point to take away in systems thinking is that nothing exists in a vacuum: Every part of training counts, affecting every other part.

Obviously, you are aware that, as a parent, you play a huge role in the system. However, it's also imperative that you *act your part accordingly* in the system. I hope that this book will give you more clarity on the matter.

Though tennis is an individual sport, in the later stages of development you will inevitably surround yourself with a team of experts – from coaches to hitting partners, sports psychologists to nutritionists. I am also a big believer in team effort when everyone knows their part well and executes the plan.

By adopting this systems thinking, your team will be better prepared to identify issues that arise and then work backward to find appropriate solutions instead of reacting compulsively and emotionally. A clear pathway will then encourage gradual efforts from every member of the team – efforts that become positive habits. I am telling you, nothing else will lead to long-term success. That's why I personally don't believe in early success. Throughout the course of this book, you will learn why.

Here is a more comprehensive quote that reflects what I am talking about:

> *"In systemic design, the methodology reflects on framing better ideas, formulating processes, generating outcomes, facilitating cooperative work,*

*and reflecting on feedback. This requires an understanding of the **interdependence of systems themselves**; the utilization of feedback loops in a non-linear fashion in order to respond accordingly; the understanding that multiple causes can result in multiple outcomes; and the ability to map it in a coherent way."*

Does all of this sound a little abstract? There are a lot of great books about systems thinking, but for an introduction I suggest reading *Thinking in Systems: A Primer* by Donella "Dana" Meadows. Though she didn't invent the concept of systems thinking, she is a master at breaking down its principles – which is sort of what I am trying to achieve with this book.

Now, let's dive into the developmental models that constitute the system.

II. Developmental Models

One of the recurring themes in my work as a coach is to introduce a little more order into the chaos that arises during practice and competition. So many variables are flying around at any one time that it is critical for young athletes to know that they can lead on expertise organized and defined in a way that helps them. One helpful approach is to compartmentalize training into general stages, such as pre-puberty, puberty, and post-puberty. There are a variety of developmental models that address the needs at each of these stages.

🎾 Côté's Developmental Model of Sports Participation

As illustrated below, this model prioritizes environmental factors over innate characteristics in talent development, connecting specific age ranges with each stage. I am personally a fan of his second path as an overall goal.

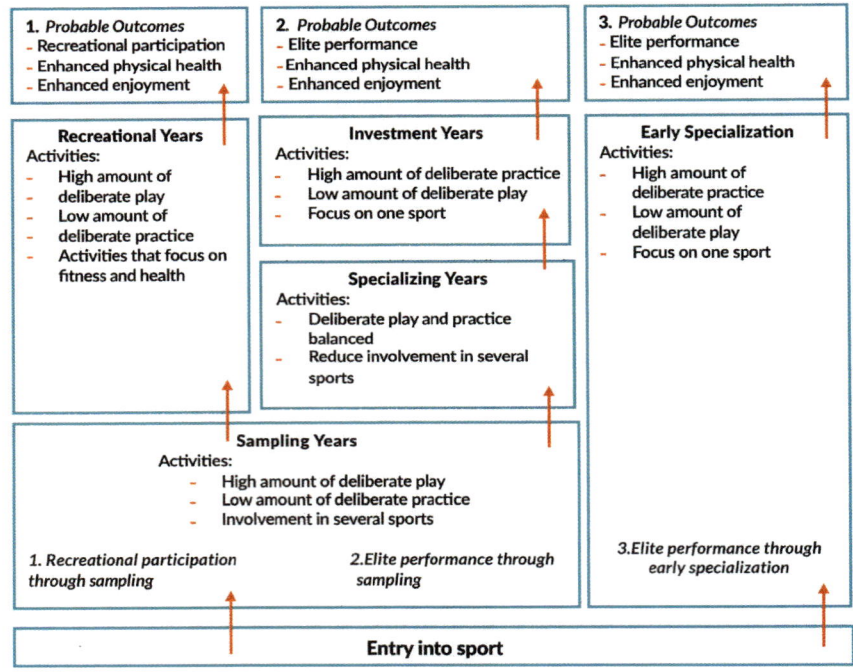

Figure 3. Côté's Developmental Model of Sports Participation

🔍 *Istvan Balyi's Long-Term Athlete Development Model*

The second model, which had a big influence on my overall philosophy as a coach, is Istvan Balyi's long-term athlete development model, or LTAD.

This is an illustration of Balyi's model.

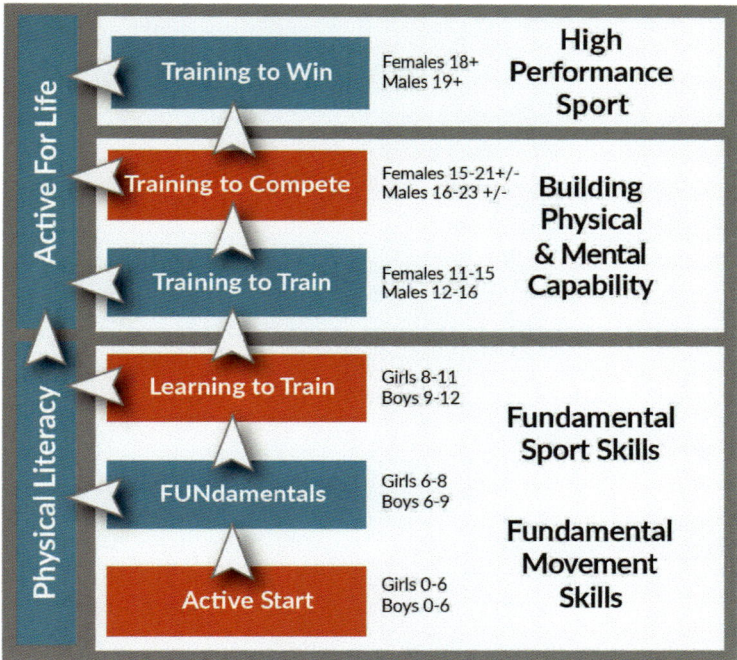

Figure 4. Istvan Balyi's Long-Term Athlete Development Model

Let's take a closer look at it.

The "**Active Start**" phase starts *literally* at birth and runs up to the age of 6. The child is starting his journey, learning to crawl, walk, and run. This is the purest form of learning.

What do I mean by that? Think back to your memory of your kid's first steps. I won't get too cliched and repetitive with the "walk before you run," but it's probably the best analogy I can provide. In tennis, the same idea applies. You have to let your kid fall, encourage him or her to get back up, and be there, holding his or her hand, making sure no skulls get cracked but showing that mistakes *can get made*. That's natural growth. That's *evolution*! So, why not apply the same philosophy to tennis?

I encourage throwing and catching at this stage to enhance the development of hand-eye coordination.

Swimming and gymnastics are *fantastic* introductory sports because they can build a strong and healthy body frame, helping to prevent muscle imbalances – especially the kind that become major issues after puberty.

I highly recommend looking for a tennis club that has implemented the "ITF Tennis 10s" pathway. This allows kids to progress along a competitive pathway according to their age, ability, confidence, and orientation to competition. In the process, the court size, racket length, ball speed, and duration of games all increase until the player is ready to move onto the full court and use a yellow ball. If you need more information, go to http://www.tennisplayandstay.com/.

This is an overview of the pathway:

Stage/Age	Ball	Ball size/Racket/Court Dimensions	Stage Description
Stage 3 **RED** 5-8 years	75% slower than a Yellow ball' (foam or Felt)	Foam ball 8.00-9.00 cm Standard ball 7.00-8.00 cm Racket 17-23"(43-58cm)** Court 36-42ft (10.97-12.8m) x 14-20ft (4.27-6.1m) Net Height (at the centre): 31.5-33' (0.8-0.838m)	• Slower balls, smaller courts and shorter rackets. • Players are able to play the game from their first lesson. • Players start to play in tennis festival events that use fun, team-based multi match events. • Development of good technique and use of realistic tactics.
Stage 2 **ORANGE** 8-10 years	50% slower than a Yellow ball'	Standard ball 6.00-6.86 cm Racket 23-25" (58-63cm)** Court 58-60ft (17.68-18.29m) x 20-27ft (6.1-8.23m) Net Height (at the centre): 31.5-36' (0.8-0.914m)	• Players move to a larger court, relevent to their size. • Ball is slightly faster than at Red, but continues to provide an optimal striking zone. • Players have the ability to implement advanced tactics. • Matches are longer than at Red, and children play both 'team' and 'individual' multi match events.
Stage 1 **GREEN** 9-10 years	20% slower than a Yellow ball'	Standard ball 6.30-6.86 cm Racket 25-26" (63-66cm)** Full Size Court 78ft (23.77) x 27ft (8.23m) Standard Net Height (at the centre): 36' (0.914m)	• The ball is faster than at Orange. • Ball still slower and lower bouncing than the yellow ball. • Experienced players are able to continue to develop good technique and to implement advanced tactics. • Matches are slightly longer than at Orange, with both 'team' and individuel' multi match competition played.
Tennis 10 years and older	Yellow ball	Standard ball 6.54-6.86 cm Racket 26-29" (66-73.7cm)** Full Size Court 78ft (23.77) x 27ft (8.23m) Standard Net Height: (at the centre): 36' (0.914m)	• Players reach Yellow having progressed through the Red, Orange and Green stages. • Players will usually be ready to train and compete with the Yellow ball on the full court.

Figure 5. **ITF Tennis 10s pathway**

The details set out in the three stages are recommendations from the ITF – which stands for the International Tennis Federation – for the development of a 10-and-under player.

Now, let's further explore the developmental stages.

1. "FUNDAMENTALS"
– ages 6 to 9 for boys and ages 6 to 8 for girls

The goal here is to develop fundamental motor skills like ***agility, balance, and coordination*** that all athletes need to master before going on to more tennis-specific skills. In this phase, the child should participate in a variety of sports besides tennis, learning to have fun while building speed, power, and endurance. This phase should cover appropriate techniques for running, jumping, and throwing to make any corrections to agility, balance, and coordination picked up during the "Active Start" phase. It should also involve strength training via bodyweight, medicine ball, and Swiss ball exercises. The key here is to explore a variety of movements. Sports parks are becoming more popular, which I think is great. The kids can explore all of these movements in a safe environment. Keep your kid active – and whatever you do, please don't let them get addicted to screens.

2. "LEARNING HOW TO TRAIN"
– ages 9 to 12 for boys and ages 8 to 11 for girls

I like to call this one **"Learning How to Learn,"** and it's probably the most important meta-skill that you can teach your kid. Learning how to learn is the ultimate superpower. This is what puts every other skill and ability within reach!

This phase will entail the continued development of fundamental motor skills, while increasing the focus on tennis-specific skills and techniques. This is where a kid should start learning to become more responsible and organized. A complete program in this phase should cover warm-ups, cool-downs, before-and-after matches and training sessions, sport-specific speed and agility development, stretching, hydration, nutrition, and basic recovery protocols. In addition, it should start introducing the notions of mental tools and routines. Much more importantly, this is where the child must be taught *why* responsibility and commitment are important.

The ratio of training-to-competition should be 70:30. If the kid plays in tournaments, the win-loss ratio should be 60:40. Yes, athletes *need* to learn how to lose as well. We will talk about this later in the sports psychology chapter.

3. "TRAINING TO TRAIN"
– *ages 12 to 16 for boys and ages 11 to 15 for girls*

This phase is all about optimizing physical capacity, emphasizing both aerobic and anaerobic conditioning, and continuing to master fundamental motor and tennis skills. This is the phase where parents and coaches try to skip ahead, thinking they might miss out. Because it's such a sensitive biological time, it can lead to *disasters*. One of the scariest pitfalls at this time is treating kids like "final products," especially the kids who reach peak height and weight faster than others, while forgetting that their brains aren't fully developed yet. Think about your computer: You don't restart it when it's installing important software. Why? Because critical damage can occur! This is also the phase when you can see the effects of the previous two phases, either positive or negative. At this point, a lot of kids quit or pause their training because of burnout or excessive injuries, while other athletes continue their development journeys. This is the stage in which to learn correct weightlifting techniques, when to taper and peak workouts, how to optimize nutrition, and how to mentally prepare for practice and competition. During this phase, I will also introduce the pre-competition, competition, and post-competition concepts into my students' lives. *The ratio of training-to-competition will shift slightly, to 60:40.*

4. "TRAINING TO COMPETE"
– *ages 16 to 18 for boys and ages 15 to 17 for girls*

By this age, the player has mastered the fundamental movement patterns if they have been addressed at the right time. Now, we can shift our focus to the **nitty-gritty of tennis**, placing more emphasis on tactics, strategies, and match analysis. On top of that, we must carefully design a fitness regimen based on individual performance diagnostics and quarterly physical evaluations. This phase should also prioritize sports psychology and more precise recovery programs. *The training-to-competition ratio should be 40:60.*

Why Tennis?

5. "TRAINING TO WIN"
– ages 18 and up for boys and ages 17 and up for girls

The "final" phase – and I put "final" in quotations because this model should be loose, personalized to each athlete – is the "Training to Win" phase, age. This is when the periodization that I will present later on plays a critical role. The top priority should be attention to detail and planning so that the athlete can peak mentally and physically in the competition.

The training-to-competition ratio should be 25:75. Because they play so many tournaments, professional tennis players dedicate most of their preparation, doing fitness in this phase, and focusing on maintaining a healthy body.

🎾 *The Dunning Kruger Effect and Noel Burch's Four Stages of Competence - UNDERSTANDING THE LEARNING CURVE*

This model offers a more realistic definition of learning, revealing the terms "danger zone" and "plateau," which many coaches, parents, and players fail to identify. Check out the illustration below, where you will see that growth is never a straight line. What feels like a plateau is part of the learning curve.

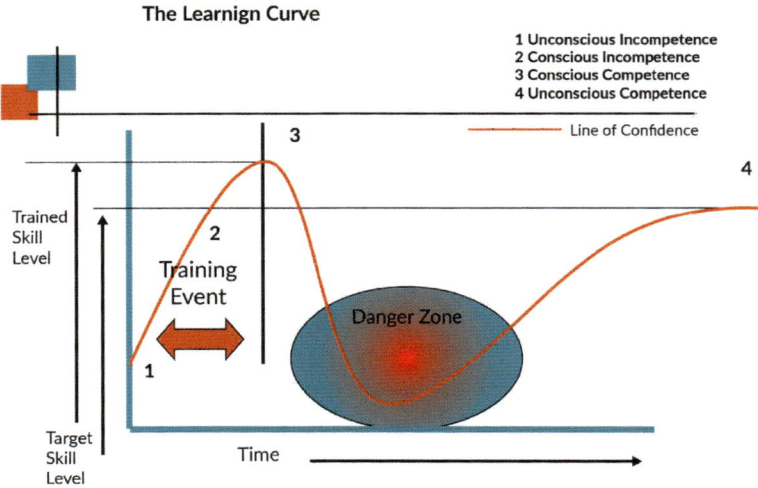

Figure 6. **The Dunning Kruger Effect - Understanding the learning curve**

This illustration makes a point that we should understand by now: Frustration can prove dangerous to athletes. That is why it is important to remember this model. Expectations should be tempered to prevent frustration from becoming burnout.

Most time spent at a skill level is spent on a plateau where you do not improve and are often frustrated. Afterwards you will improve lot then get a little worse and return to another plateau; which is an improvement to your previous plateau.

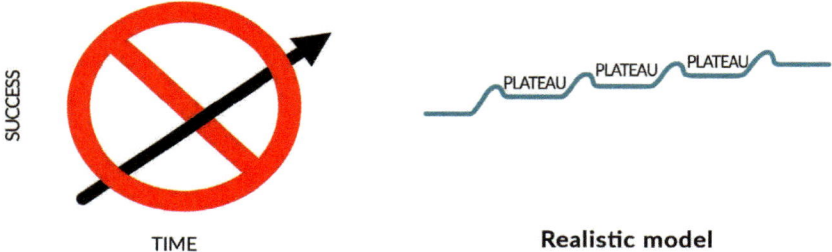

Realistic model

One of the most destructive things we can do is to "fast track." More times than I would care to admit, I have seen tennis players trying to ignore the developmental models and train as if they were in a phase that they were not in. No matter which model we use, we should remain aware of the fact that the most important concept is *patience*. I understand that, as a parent, you want to make sure you're doing everything you can. However, sometimes that "*I need to do something, or I need to change something*" urge can be very detrimental to a child's growth. The way I see it, *patience is also a form of action*. So, you have two choices: (1) Always making changes to the system, never following through, and always chasing the newest fads, or (2) Finding patience and filling your role properly. In the end, your choice will have a tremendous effect on your kid's future and character, i.e., whether or not he or she will become the next Nadal or Serena. Like I said, becoming successful as a tennis player should always be a byproduct of this educational journey.

Of course, each person's biology differs. This is why personalization will play an important role in the end. All of these are general models. They're not *prescriptive*. Rather, they're **descriptive**, offering a basis from which to create a framework for training. I am just making you aware of their existence. When you feel frustrated or in doubt, look to their suggestions, and *never* skip a stage.

Next, let's look at the fundamentals that underpin all these models.

III. Physical Literacy

You can practice shooting eight hours a day, but if your technique is wrong, then all you become is very good at shooting the wrong way. **Get the fundamentals down and the level of everything you do will rise.**

~ Michael Jordan

The physicality in modern tennis is increasing at a breakneck pace. To keep up, one must understand physical literacy. I hope this book will teach you that, because if there is one thing an elite tennis player can't lack, it's the fundamentals – which start with general physical development. More and more tennis players are specializing too soon and dropping out quicker because they're missing out on this. It's time to emphasize **player health and development first and foremost**.

I need you to understand this: To become a great tennis player, a kid must first become a great athlete. When you hear this said aloud, it may seem obvious. In practice, though, it is anything *but* obvious. All the time, I see kids struggle for reasons that are both outside their control and wholly avoidable. Again, I am not talking about genetics here. It comes down to properly teaching and coaching fundamental techniques, thereby giving children the confidence boost they need to maximize their potential.

So, before we can talk about anything else, we need to understand why all of this information is important. I always like to start at the very beginning and then move forward, so let's start at the ***foundations of human movement***. These include jumping, throwing, receiving, kicking, catching, climbing, bounding, tumbling, and skipping. We use them to build up to more specialized movements. After training dozens of gifted, promising 12-year-olds who couldn't skip or leapfrog correctly (just to give you an example), I can tell you, with no hesitation, that this matters tremendously and it's far too often overlooked! Fail to learn the ***foundational skills***, and the results echo throughout the rest of the learning process, leading to premature dropouts and injuries. Intuitively, we *know* that we need to build on our skills, mastering the less-complex ones before we can use them as the basis for more complex ones. But often, when we feel frustrated or overwhelmed, we can lose sight of this idea.

Why does this happen? It's simple: Parents are so dead-set on seeing their kids win *immediately* that they push and push and push – right into a sinkhole. All of that hard work goes straight down the drain, and I can't even begin to tell you how many sleepless nights this has caused me. The only solution is *patience through structure*. There is just no way around that.

This chart illustrates what I am trying to tell you about the fundamentals:

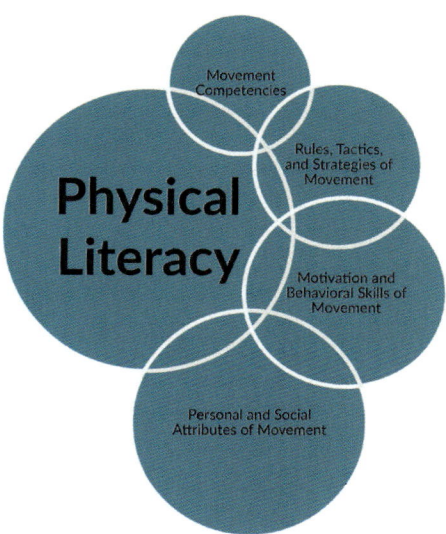

Figure 7. **Physical Literacy and its developmental branches**

You see how physical literacy leads into other developmental areas? This is the way it *has* to be. Learning physical literacy and establishing proper motor competency *first* will facilitate the exploration and implementation of the technical side of higher-level tennis. To give you a popular example of something I've noticed over the years: The serve is arguably one of the most complex skills to master in tennis. As a coach, I find it very difficult to teach a kid how to serve before he or she has a basic notion of throwing. If a kid learns how to throw a baseball, football, or any type of ball when he or she is younger, that child will more easily pick up all of the more complex ideas that *build* off throwing. Try teaching a kid quantum mechanics before he or she learns basic physics. It is just *not* going to happen. This is a **long-term specialization sport** that not only requires but relies on the athlete's immersion in fundamental movement literacy from an early age, both on and off the tennis court.

From everything that I have seen throughout my career, the kids who have a higher rate of success as athletes are the ones who master the fundamentals at an early age. They flow more smoothly on the tennis court, which boosts their confidence and frees them up to learn and even get creative in their game. You see more enjoyment on their faces when they're out there playing. They're immersed, and they are actually *playing tennis*. As a parent, you may feel impatient when you are watching your younger child fumble through the basics. Just trust me on this: Progress *will* start to show. If you give the process time, you will see it pay off. The benefits of **mastering the fundamentals** are tremendous.

The kids whose coaches and parents pressure them to win at an early age end up falling short of their potential later on. Focusing too much on tournaments at an early age limits the overall development, especially in the later stages. I've seen it way too many times. The *only* focus for a child should be learning and growing at his or her own pace. Those who do not embrace the process and do not faithfully follow it inevitably run into burnout, chronic injury, and premature developmental issues.

For tennis players ages 12, 10, and below, physical literacy is *critical*. The same is true for athletes at every level; however, for athletes who have not built up years of experience, the focus should be on overall athleticism, fundamental movement, and motor skills. I want to emphasize something here: If kids have not developed proper fundamental motor and skills by the age of 12, the opportunity has passed. I am not trying to scare you, but once the window of opportunity has passed, it is gone. Add to that the fact that this window of opportunity is directly connected to a sound technical foundation in tennis. I can't stress this enough. To cover it fully, I'd need to write a whole other book about it. If your kid is allowed to properly learn fundamental human movements, it's easier for me to teach him or her the proper techniques specific to tennis. *That* can be the difference between good and elite.

Now, is remediation possible later on? Sure, it's possible. It's possible you will pick up French in your adult years and then become a famous French author, too – but extremely unlikely. Miss the window and kids have to play catch-up instead of getting ahead of the game, usually overcompensating to the point of over-training, frustration, and injury.

As you previously saw in the Istvan Balyi's long-term athletic development (**LTAD**) model, it connects directly to the "age constraints" that I am referring to here. Through the LTAD model, we are leveraging biological training windows and cultivating skills during the times when those skills match up with physical development.

So, what is physical literacy? It is about thinking of kids as athletes *first* and *then* as tennis players. That is the only order that I know to make sense and the only order that will lead to positive outcomes. You have to think about this from the ground up!

Let's move from the body to the mind, to understand how the two are inextricably connected.

IV. Sports Psychology

Take any elite athlete in the world, current or past, and read their biography. You will notice that they're always crediting their success to the *power of the mind*. LeBron James, Michael Jordan, Kobe Bryant, Cristiano Ronaldo, Conor McGregor, Tiger Woods, Serena Williams, Venus Williams, Novak Djokovic, Rafael Nadal – shall I keep going? It's the same story. Across every sport, top athletes all seem to have common mental tools that they're using. One of them is ***visualization***. They've all developed this acute sense of seeing things happen in their minds long before those things become realities. And we, as parents and teachers, can have such a big influence in terms of either enhancing or limiting that sense in a child.

Are they all committed, too? Sure. They draw that from within themselves, though. As Richard Williams, father of Serena and Venus, said, "A parent must *allow* the child to be committed. Don't be committed for them." This is a powerful point, and it's easy to miss.

Commitment is only the beginning. On top of this are all the delicate and more subtle ways of interpreting reality that kids will eventually depict throughout their childhood and adolescence – like *abundance versus scarcity* and *inspiration versus desperation*. Most of these will stem from *what and how* we communicate – both verbally and non-verbally – with kids on a daily basis as they are growing up. If the kid is in a scarcity mindset and desperate for success at an early age, it will not end well – I guarantee you that. One way or another, sooner or later, disaster is on the horizon. I'm not saying that I am against instilling a winner's mentality from a young age. I am just trying to shed some light on the difference between desperation and inspiration and how kids interpret reality. How do you expect your kid to eventually train five to six hours daily at maximum intensity (which is the norm in modern tennis) if he or she is not inspired?

Was Kobe Bryant obsessed with winning? Absolutely, and even though he had to overcome major adversities, it came from a place of inspiration, from a place of abundance. Why? Because it came from within himself. That's why I want my players' mentality to be *I want to win* instead of *I need to win*. Winning is subordinate to inspiration and learning, to growth and mastery, to process orientation. What I want more than that is for my kids to cultivate **curiosity, self-reliance, and inquisitiveness**. If your kid is constantly seeking your approval or the coach's approval, that is not the right track. When you put a label on a kid, you are creating a limitation – because the label *becomes* the limitation. We must use our words carefully because these can, in turn, become the child's internal words. On the bright side, the right words can help us build a strong mental perspective that comes from a place of **abundance and inspiration**, which we can then use as a launchpad to talk about the actual techniques of sports psychology.

Conor McGregor, although controversial, is one of my favorite UFC fighters. I enjoy studying his training methods overall, and I am fascinated by his mindset. One of my favorite quotes of his that has stuck with me is *"You either WIN or you LEARN."* Another fascinating thing about Conor is that he readily admits that he uses the law of attraction to win. How? Simply put, he believes that *"We attract into our lives what we think about most of the time, good or bad."* When you're thinking confident thoughts and making confident statements, like Conor always is, then you make success your destiny. You combine ultra-confidence with ultra-gratitude. As he says, *"You need to appreciate your surroundings and be grateful for it, and that's when good things happen. To have that bitterness and negativity, that's when things go bad. I think the fact that I appreciate everything and that I'm grateful for the things around me, that's why it's going so good for me."*

Conor doesn't play "not to lose." Why? Because his mindset is "win or *learn*." He visualizes good things happening for him in both good and bad times. Again, in his words, **"Visualizing good things in times of struggle, when you can do that, that really makes the law of attraction work."**

Do you see how all of these mindsets that Conor is cultivating lead to the absence of the fear of failure? As a parent, you must help your kid reach this point, too. Believe me: There is enough fear of failure. I've seen too much of it and it's one of the leading causes of early dropouts in tennis and sports in general. Losing and failure are *not* the same. We – as parents, teachers, and coaches – have a tremendous power to influence that mentality from an early age, in either a good way or a bad way. I have had my share of mistakes and learning experiences, which is why I take this responsibility *very* seriously.

Michael Jordan says something similar about fear: *"Limits, like fear, is often an illusion."*

If you are still struggling to accept losing as a *positive* because of the opportunity it presents, there it is, in these quotes. Fear of failure or disappointment is an *illusion* that is, in most parts, constructed by the most influencing people in a child's life – parents, family, teachers, and coaches. From a child's perspective, this can become overwhelming if it is not handled carefully. We often mess up by creating these fears and limitations in kids' heads by comparing them to other kids or by imposing our authority as adults too much just because we had a bad day. It adds up over time. Plus, they are *completely* dependent on us to teach them what matters, what to focus on, and how the world works.

If you are being more loving than usual after a victory or showing your kid your disappointment after a tough loss, you are basically teaching him or her that your love and approval are conditional. Then, your kid will think of tennis as something that's conditional too. Sooner or later, this will have negative repercussions. So, I strongly recommend that your questions after a match revolve around your child and not the outcome. Focus on effort instead of results. Never ask "Did you win?" Or "What was the score?" Instead, it is better to ask "What did you learn?" or "How did you play?" Make your kid realize that you are more interested in him or her than the result. By doing so, you are encouraging independence. Before we can demand hard work and relentlessness, we must create the right mindset.

Now, before we move on, let me put all of this into perspective. These athletes who I'm quoting were born with tremendous genetics. I would never argue that they weren't. Your kid, through practice alone, will probably never achieve Federer's genius, and I would not want to convince you that talent is irrelevant. Talent *is* relevant. Anyone who says otherwise is *lying*. I didn't write this book to try to make you think that talent is a myth. What matters to me is what we can do with talent. How can we maximize the talent that is available? That's a different ball game.

Now, let's shift back to tennis specifically. Today, the majority of top ATP and WTA players communicate with sports psychologists often. Although their specific goals in working with a sports psychologist may vary, they often quote the same general motivations: **mental toughness, mental preparation, attention, motivation, and optimal function.**

This chart illustrates how mental health plays into all areas of life and training.

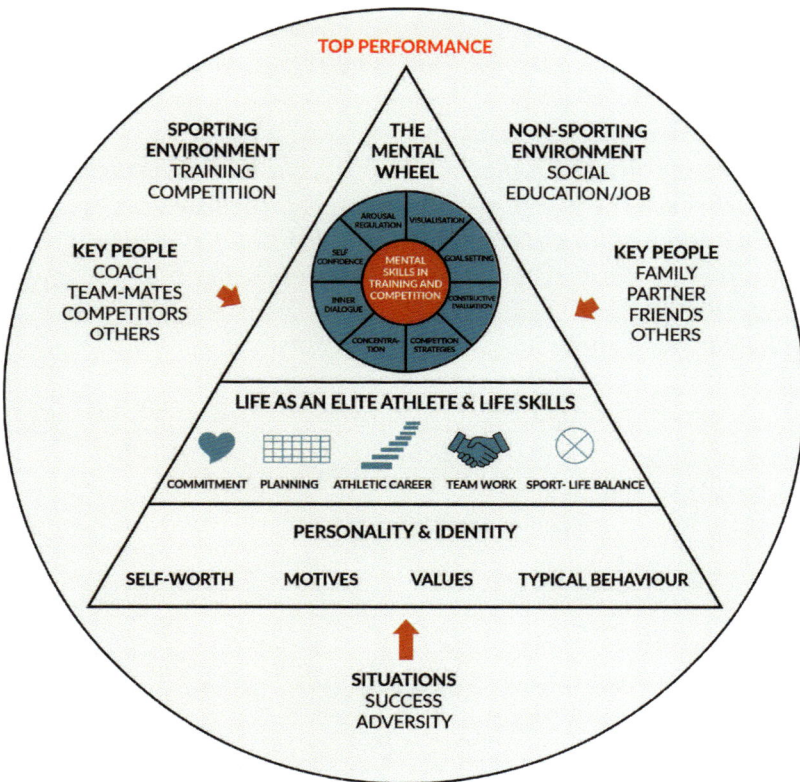

Figure 8. **The Mental Wheel Pyramid.**

I am a big fan of Csikszentmihalyi, who concluded that sports psychology techniques can enable the athlete to navigate anxiety and focus more effectively during practice and competition, leading to higher performance levels – and easier access to the all-important *flow state*. This is a state of mind that athletes achieve when they feel completely engaged in their performance, losing perception of time and concentrating on the moment. As any athlete will tell you, it's where peak performance happens. I personally stumbled into flow totally by mistake when I used to play the sport. I had no idea how to harness it, but when I figured it out, it was bliss. Tennis became enjoyable for me, I became more immersed in it, I made more progress, and I saw better results. It seemed organic. It was too late, though. That's why I am so motivated about my job – to give kids a better chance from the start and avoid having to play catch-up when they grow up. Yes, hard work is important. It's one of my mantras. But the truth is, if the kid has zero enjoyment, then something is fundamentally wrong in the system. Without *flow*, there's no way to reach full potential. I don't care how many forehands a day your kid is hitting or what supplement he or she is taking.

So, who is Csikszentmihalyi and *what is fun or enjoyment*? To give you an overview, he is one of the top psychologists of his generation, and he's important to us here because of his concept of enjoyment in order to pursue mastery. He viewed it as a process that occurs when **high challenges and skills are matched**. This diagram shows you what he's talking about:

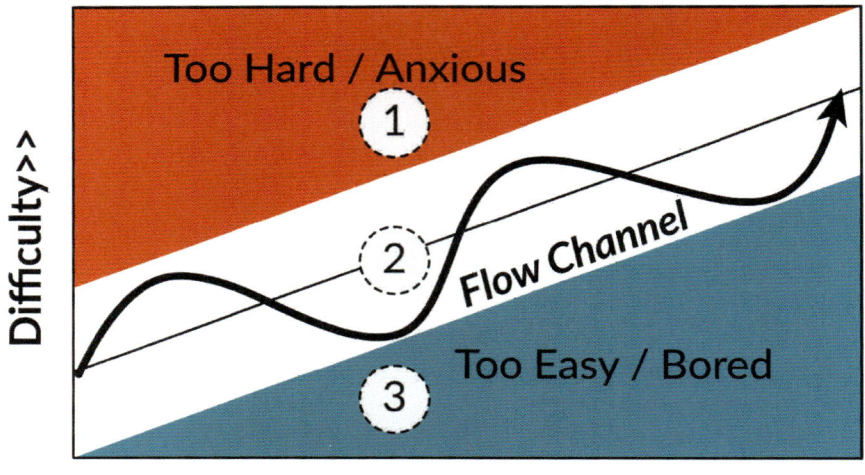

Figure 9. Csikszentmihalyi's flow channel model

I think that parents and coaches should use this as a monitoring tool to. This is the catalyst for all the other elements to interact and work more efficiently.

Now, let me define what *fu*n should mean for any aspiring professional athlete. Don't confuse *fun* with a generic term for goofing around. That's not what I'm talking about. Sports psychology is not merely about *feeling* good. That can help, but I want it to be more. It *has* to be more, and Csikszentmihalyi would agree. When fun equates to flow state, we see real magic in athletes. That is what sports psychology is unlocking.

Today, top coaches know without a doubt that tennis players can set themselves up for more consistent results by undergoing a daily or weekly mental preparation program, collaborating with a sports psychologist. Parents and coaches will play a massive role in this collaboration, with the sports psychologist facilitating the parent-coach-player triad that is integral throughout training.

One of the books that I always recommend, as an introduction to the mental side of tennis, is called *The Inner Game of Tennis*, written by Timothy Gallwey.

In conclusion: You must be able to determine when your kid is deviating from *flow state*, and you must separate that from giving up when things are too hard (the militaristic approach) or too easy (when we give medals for tenth place).

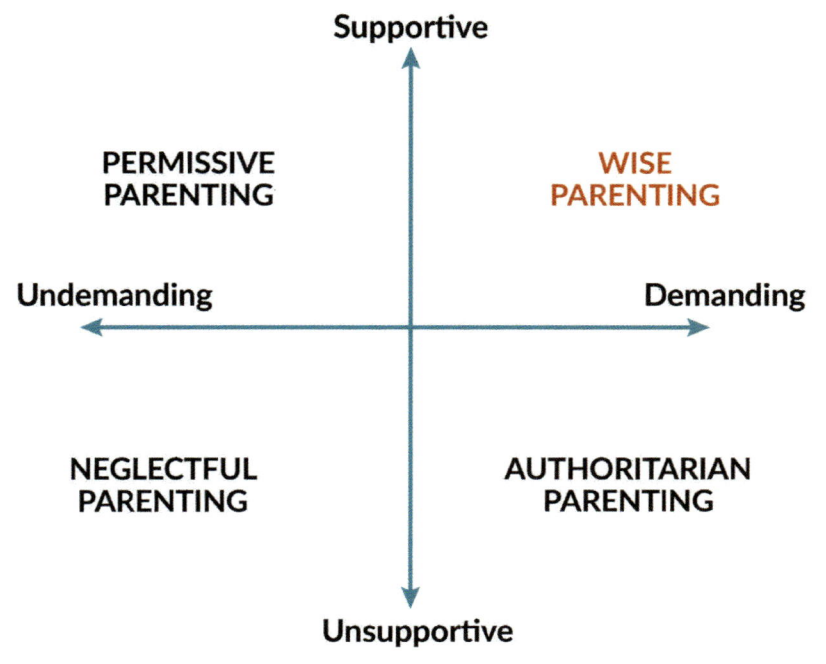

	Supportive	
PERMISSIVE PARENTING		**WISE PARENTING**
Undemanding		**Demanding**
NEGLECTFUL PARENTING		**AUTHORITARIAN PARENTING**
	Unsupportive	

Figure 10. **Duckworth model of parenting in sports**

V. Nutrition and Hydration

To understand how tremendously nutrition can affect an athlete, we only need to look at tennis superstar Novak Djokovic. In 2010, he was viewed as an upcoming superstar. However, at the same time, he was running out of gas in the middle of matches. I remember a lot of "experts" at the time saying, "He doesn't have what it takes or it was just his personality." It took a nutritionist to spot this and start formulating some theories. The conclusion? Djokovic was struggling through an undiagnosed gluten sensitivity, which was throwing his entire body out of whack. Maybe this should give you some perspective on where I am coming from when I tell you to stop ignoring the "minor details."

While these circumstances were exceptional, few tennis players are following nutrition and diet plans that are ideal for their bodies. Every meal impacts performance on the court. The wrong meal can lead to injuries and subpar development, while the right meal can lead to strength and growth.

Before we look at the specific nutrition pitfalls that tennis players encounter, let's define sports nutrition in general. Defined as the study and practice of diet with regard to improving athletic performance, sports nutrition is useful for anyone who is trying to build strength and endurance. It asks questions like "Which fluids and foods should an athlete consume?" and "How much of each fluid and food is appropriate?" It also considers the specific vitamins, minerals, supplements, carbohydrates, proteins, and fats that athletes require to train and compete efficiently at peak capacity.

One thing that I always state up front is that parents must learn more about basic fluid and nutrition requirements, even if they are not going to become experts in the field. For a kid to develop into a high-performance athlete, you *cannot* confuse general nutrition with **sports nutrition**.

The first point to consider is protein, which most tennis players miss out on, emphasizing carb-loading instead. While carb-loading is useful in some situations, it falls short of a complete strategy, which includes *all three* macronutrients (proteins, carbohydrates, and essential fats). By consuming all three macronutrients in proper quantities, athletes can optimize their training recovery and growth.

Remember that even if we are not lifting weights in the middle of tennis practice, we are still putting immense stress on our bodies. This breaks down muscle – and to recover and build muscle, the body *needs* protein. Of equal importance to protein sufficiency is *calorie balance* – how much an athlete eats versus how much he or she burns. So, make sure your kid eats enough!

Check out this breakdown of the importance of every component in a diet.

Comparing Magnitudes

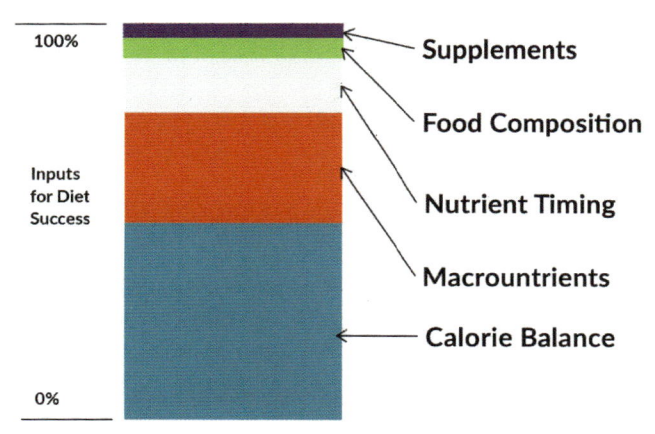

Figure 11. **Matt Kuzdub's Calorie Balance chart for professional athletes**

I combine all of these concepts into the nutritional plans that I develop for juniors. This is a nutritional plan that I tailored to one of my students. She is 12 years old, plays tennis for around four hours per day, and, without proper nutrition, would be at serious risk of injury – and never even approach her true developmental potential.

	Monday	Tuesday	Wednesday	Thursday	Friday	Saturday	Sunday
Breakfast	• 3 egg omelet with avocados and some seeds (chia, hemp, flax) • Chocolate milk	• Oatmeal • 2 different colored fruits	• Veggie omelette with some cheese on whole wheat toast • Chocolate milk	• Protein pancakes • 2 different colored fruits	• Oatmeal • 2 different colored fruits	• Veggie omelette with some cheese on whole wheat toast • Chocolate milk	• Protein pancakes • 2 different colored fruits
Snack 1	• Fruit with nuts	• Cliff bar	• Blueberry Fruit smoothie with some nuts	• Mixed vegetable/juice smoothie	• Protein shake	• Fruit with nuts	• Cliff bar
Lunch	• Grilled chicken with quinoa and mixed greens • Lemon water	• Steak with brown rice sprinkle some turmeric • Electrolyte drink	• Grilled Wild caught salmon with some olive oil, mixed greens	• Grilled chicken with quinoa and mixed greens • Lemon water	• Steak with brown rice sprinkle some turmeric • Electrolyte drink	• Grilled Wild caught salmon with some olive oil, mixed greens	• Shrimp Tacos with quinoa and black beans • Lemon water
Snack 2	• Yogurt / kefir	• Protein shake	• Yogurt / kefir	• Cliff bar	• Yogurt / kefir	• Her favorite snack	• Mixed vegetable/juice smoothie
Dinner	• Tuna fish • Cherry Tart Juice	• Turkey meatballs with some spaghetti • Cherry tart juice	• Garlic Shrimp with quinoa and avocado • Cherry tart juice	• Tuna fish burger on whole what bread Cherry Tart Juice	• Veggic balls with some spaghetti • Cherry tart juice	• Bison Burger with cheese and avocados • Sweet potatoes • Cherry tart juice	• Tuna fish Cherry Tart Juice

Figure 12. **Nutritional plan template**

Now, eating enough, eating the right foods, selecting the right protein powders, selecting the right probiotics – is that it? Unfortunately, it is *not*. Consulting a sports nutritionist can take some of the guesswork out of this often-complex equation, which will vary greatly from one athlete to the next. This can be extremely useful in the more advanced and competitive stages of development. Also, knowing whether your kid is allergic to certain types of foods, or is lacking certain nutrients in his or her body, can have a great impact on the child's overall mental and physical performance.

One thing that will remain constant across all athletes, regardless of age, gender, or genetic predispositions, is **hydration**. During training sessions of an hour or less, athletes can get away with simply drinking water to maintain hydration levels, even if the session is in the heat.

Most juniors below the age of 12 will *never* need anything more than water unless they are playing in extreme conditions. However, for longer sessions and older athletes, water may not be enough. In hot and humid climates in particular, athletes may need to supplement water with electrolytes and carbohydrates.

When shopping around for electrolytes, you may find yourself drawn to commercial sports drinks. I would tell you to stop where you are and put them down immediately because the glucose concentration is *way* too high. This can do more harm than good. My suggestion is simple: Squeeze some lemon into the water for a boost of vitamin C, potassium, calcium, and magnesium, along with added flavor. That's it. I was very much into "sports drinks" until a sports nutritionist gave me a reality check, telling me how harmful it can be to a kid.

So, how much hydration is enough? A good rule of thumb, and what I always tell my students, is *"Don't wait to get thirsty."*

Food is the more complicated side of nutrition. What you can do to make this simpler is *make sure your kid eats enough before seeing the sports nutritionist*. By remaining cognizant of both these variables, athletes can help prevent injuries and cramps, function better, perform better, and also think better because high-quality food leads to stronger cognition.

What's also important to understand is that stomach function impacts mood, alertness, and performance in children. This is why I consider nutrition and hydration to be an extended branch of the recovery protocols. Let's look at this topic a little more in-depth.

VI. Recovery Protocols – The Key to Longevity

I hear the term "over-training" a lot these days. This term has become more popular in recent years. I would compare it to the word "gluten": Everyone is talking about it, but the majority have no idea what it is. I'm not saying it's bad that people are talking about "over-training," but I think we need to identify it better so that we can address it properly.

The truth is, in the majority of cases, "over-training" is under-recovery. To fully understand this statement, you *need* to look at the **underlying causes**. You need to put this into the whole system that we are talking about here, instead of blaming one isolated event on long-term failures. Typically, the true cause of burnout is not over-training but, rather, ***under-recovering***. Under the right conditions, an athlete's body is resilient, capable of withstanding tremendous stress, which we define as any work the body does. However, the right conditions are never possible without proper recovery protocols. I firmly believe that most athletes can train *harder* than they are currently, if only they were paying more attention to their recovery.

The vast majority of the time, parents and coaches overlook or ignore the training-recovery protocols that must occur off the tennis court – undermining the strict curfew, letting their children sit around on their phones for too long, and serving up junk food, to name just a few "minor details."

The most important of all the recovery protocols is something we already do: sleep.

Maybe you are thinking *I already sleep, and I understand it's important*. We all sleep, sure, but few of us are diligent about the quality and timing of our sleep. Athletes need to sleep between eight and ten hours every single night, depending on age. This should become a routine. A recent study out of Harvard Medical School found that, contrary to popular belief, you cannot "catch up" on sleep that you have missed in a night. Let's bust that myth *right now*.

It is also common for kids to get the right amount of sleep but miss out on proper quality. Young athletes who sleep for eight, nine, or ten hours a night but experience poor sleep quality are at a noteworthy disadvantage. We see this in our own lives. When we wake up feeling groggy, we can usually point to a likely cause: poor sleep quality.

One of the key causes of poor sleep quality among juniors is the overuse of phones, tablets, and other devices. The blue light that these devices emit can delay the production of melatonin, which is the hormone responsible for the sleep-wake cycle regulation. This, in turn, raises the cortisol levels, which naturally rise in the 30 to 60 minutes after waking, leading to a complete break in the circadian rhythm, much as it would if someone were to try to sleep under the sun in the middle of the day. Because of blue light's short wavelength, it harms melatonin production more than any other type of wavelength, meaning that kids who are on their devices too much will experience less REM sleep. The solution is to implement strict time limits and curfews for all devices. There is no arguing with these limits and curfews any more than there is arguing about the way to hold a tennis racket, as the limits and curfews are *necessary* for proper training.

I use the term "recovery protocols" to refer to a range of strategies and techniques that athletes can use to keep themselves running efficiently and avoid injury. Some of these, like yoga and meditation, may seem new to some athletes. They can be extremely useful, though. And they're becoming increasingly popular among professional athletes. LeBron James is one major example. In addition to taking serious precautions to protect his body and ensure his longevity, he also integrates mental and emotional preparation into the equation. Meditation is a big part of that.

Meditation is one form of rest. Unfortunately, it has a bad reputation because, again, it's poorly understood. It looks a lot like boredom to the untrained eye, but you have to see it as *rest for the mind*, freeing it from the stress of excessive cognitive stimulation. Sadly, the modern world doesn't foster a healthy environment for the brain. Over-stimulation is almost universal. Jim Kwick, the writer of the fantastic book *LIMITLESS,* indicts the four "growing villains" that are challenging our capacity to *think, focus, learn, grow, and be fully human*. Here is an excerpt from his book that I think will better illustrate what I am trying to say:

> *The first growing villain is **digital deluge**— the unending flood of information in a world of finite time and unfair expectations that leads to overwhelm, anxiety, and sleeplessness. Drowning in data and rapid change, we long for strategies and tools to regain some semblance of productivity, performance, and peace of mind.*
>
> *The second villain is **digital distraction**. The fleeting ping of digital dopamine pleasure replaces our ability to sustain the attention necessary for deep relationship, deep learning, or deep work. I recently sat next to a friend at a lecture and noticed her picking up her phone multiple times within a few minutes. I asked for her phone and pulled up the screen time app. She had picked her phone more than one thousand times and had one thousand notifications in one day. Texts, social media notifications, e-mails, and news alerts, while important in context, can derail our concentration and train us to be distracted from what matters most in the moment.*

*The third villain is **digital dementia**. Memory is a muscle that we have allowed to atrophy. While there are benefits to having a supercomputer in your pocket, think of it like an electric bicycle. It's fun and easy but doesn't get you in shape. Research on dementia proves that the greater our capacity to learn— the more mental "brainercise" we perform— the lower our risk of dementia. In many cases, we have outsourced our memory to our detriment.*

*The last brain-damaging villain is **digital deduction**. In a world where information is abundantly accessible, we've perhaps gone too far in how we use that information, even getting to the point where we are letting technology do much of our critical thinking and reasoning for us. Online, there are so many conclusions being drawn by others that we have begun to surrender our own ability to draw conclusions. We would never let another person do our thinking for us, but we've gotten far too comfortable with letting devices have that very power. The cumulative effects of these four digital villains robs us of our focus, attention, learning, and, most importantly, our ability to truly think. It robs us of our mental clarity and results in brain fatigue, distraction, inability to easily learn, and unhappiness. While the technological advances of our time have the potential to both help and harm, the way we use them in our society can lead to an epidemic of overload, memory loss, distraction, and dependency. And it's only going to get worse. Your kids were born with the ultimate technology, and there is nothing more important than the health and fitness of our brain— it controls everything in life."*

Scientific evidence backs up the impact of meditation. As Kristen Race, who holds a PhD in psychology and runs *Mindful Life Today*, says, "If you look at functional MRI scans of meditators, you see increased stimulation in the prefrontal cortex, you see a thickening of the gray matter. You see a shrinking of the amygdala which is responsible for the flight or fight response." As Dr. Race describes it, the prefrontal cortex is the "more sophisticated" part of the brain. This is where we make decisions, solve problems, and respond to stress. Meditation strengthens it, like exercise strengthens other muscles.

One specific piece of advice: At least one day per week, let your kid empty the mind. Meditation can be very useful, and it can really balance the mind-body connection. This is something I strongly believe will be a big part of everyone's life in the near future. So, even though it may seem counter-intuitive, it's a positive thing if, every once in a while, your kid is telling you that he or she is bored. Why? Because boredom is the mind's chance to take a break from all the overload. So, how about more meditation and less digital stimulation for the brain? It will have a tremendous impact on your kid's overall behavior.

Yoga can also have tremendous benefits in terms of keeping the mind and body limber and loose, which frees up the athlete to train more efficiently and more often. When an athlete practices yoga, he or she will be in better touch with the body and more attuned to what it can handle. This can lead sequentially to flow, more enjoyment, progress, and results. I am trying to re-emphasize the importance of the interconnectedness of all the elements.

I hope that if you take these fundamental and key concepts, which I have carefully selected, you can sift through the data more intelligently. From there, you can develop new methods and skills for dealing with the endless distractions in our world.

In conclusion, stress + rest = *growth*! Simply put, we don't improve a skill or any other biomotor quality through training alone. We improve these qualities by **recovering from a training stimulus**.

For all of these protocols, I want you to erase the idea that *more is better*. Higher *quality* is better. Then, the *quantity* of *quality* is better. That's what I want to see! If it's not quality, we want less, not more. Do you see that? There's an example in which more *isn't* better.

You can't have one without the other!

If the stimulus is too low, the kids remain where they are in their development or even start to lose some of their progress. Without rest, though, athletes hit a wall, failing to grow at all, no matter how hard they are working. The key is to *balance* these two parts.

VII. Periodization and Planning

Imagine if you tried to build a house without a plan. Would you expect everything to go as you wanted? Of course not. We *know* that we must approach highly-involved projects with some sort of blueprint that moves us from one point to the next. Often, however, tennis players and coaches dive into training without any plan at all, choosing drills, exercises, and workouts at random.

Needless to say, this is not how the elites approach their training. The best players and coaches think out a structure before ever stepping onto the court. I arrange the entire season around tournament schedules, training goals, and individual needs. This is called "periodization," and it involves **systematic planning and training**.

There is no way around sports periodization for any athlete who is looking to achieve peak performance. To work around competition and training, we need to implement progressive cycling. One type of cycling breaks a training program into segments: off-season, preseason, in-season, and postseason, dividing the year according to goals, as Arnd Krüger explains.

This is a breakdown of one periodization plan.

Phases of training	Prepatory			Competitive		Transition
Sub-phases	General preparation	Specific preparation	Pre-competitive	Competitive		Transition
Macro-cycles						
Micro-cycles						

Figure 13. **Division of an annual plan into its phases and cycles of training**

It may seem convoluted on the surface, but in practice, it *frees* the athlete from any confusion, providing direction from one training session to the next. Many people wrongly believe that players who are 12, 10, and younger do not need to abide by sports periodization ... but *they do*. During the earliest stages of development, appropriate training is of utmost importance, not only instilling the right habits and mindsets but conditioning the body for more advanced training.

Here's what I need you to realize. Tennis training is abstract, unpredictable, and hard to plan. Even more than other sports, it trips up young athletes. I see kids spending way too much time in specific and competitive phases, and it just crushes them. They get hurt, they burn themselves out, and then where are we? We've wasted *years*. Deviations happen, but that's still no excuse to drop planning altogether. We need a structure; otherwise, we're not going to see the progress we want. Without structure, you get confusion, which is the last thing you want. I learned that the hard way myself. That is why I want you to have a basic notion of what periodization is.

Now, let's shift our attention to the science behind all of this.

VIII. Sports Science

The way you prepare for tennis is about to change!

You're not a scientist? That's *fine*! You can still use science (the *right* science) to play your role in your child's development as an athlete.

Sports science is much more than the abstraction of sports concepts. At its core, it is about ***performance diagnostics***. Many elite players face the same problems: haphazard plans, unstructured workouts, no way to track and quantify progress. I blame it on the coaches here. We have to provide better and more accurate feedback about the kid's progress to a parent. If we don't, parents will get impatient and frustrated, and, in the majority of cases, will revert to the easiest indicator of progress that they know: tournament results. You see where I'm going with this.

Using sports science, we have reached a new pinnacle in the development of the human body. This explains, at least in part, why so many athletes are breaking old records and setting new ones – year after year. To study how the healthy human body works during exercise and how physical activity promotes holistic health, we turn to a variety of academic fields, including physiology, psychology, and anatomy – even physics, engineering, and chemistry. The goal is always the same, though: results. Whenever sports science seems a little lofty, remind yourself of that. *All of this* is contributing to the *long-term* results that we have in mind.

Take the Sports Science Lab (https://nysportssciencelab.com/), with which I have worked closely for a few years now. They are integrating science, innovation, and personalized training to **develop athletes more effectively and more efficiently**. Their thinking flies in the face of the one-size-fits-all approach to sports that has run rampant for decades. If you look at the top athletes and teams, you will invariably find that they are thinking in this way – how to make their training more specialized and leave one-size-fits-all in the past, where it belongs.

Some of the techniques that the Sports Science Lab uses are 3D kinematic and motion analysis for identifying movement patterns and muscle imbalances and analytical tools for neurological, musculoskeletal, and aerobic capacity. I know this may sound too pretentious or technical, but I don't view this type of work as "extra": It's not something an athlete can do to try to find a small edge. Rather, this work is – and should be – at the front of everyone's minds. It is *critical* in the training process for all modern athletes. This modern game of tennis is incredibly demanding, which means that sports science is a *must*. You must pay attention to this stuff or it's going to come back and create headaches for you later. As I said, I want to help you prevent the pain and struggle that catch-up always entails. Learn the concepts now so that they can work for you later.

Sports science addresses one of the most vicious problems that any aspiring tennis player faces. It is the lack of information that *always* comes back to haunt players more than they would expect! Struggling to find enough data and insight, athletes fall into the same old traps, from chronic injury to more frequent accidents to steeper learning curves to irregular performance. In a sense, sports science takes the chaos of the tennis court and gives it some structure during the practice and training phases. The tennis coach can gain a lot of insight from all of this data, which leads to more productive training.

Think about injury reduction, performance enhancement, and true technical mastery. Can I help a junior achieve all these things through hard work alone? Hard work is certainly part of the equation for inspiration, but there is another part of it. *Smart work* is just as important as hard work, if not more important. That is what sports science is. It is smart work, based on empirical evidence, plain and simple. Without it, tennis training falls apart long before the first point in a match. I suggest that you look into it deeply and then, together with your coach, try to integrate it into your child's development.

IX. Athlete Management

I see this as a never-ending process, of course. If we want to see progress, both as people and as tennis players, we must understand and study the interactions between the child and his or her immediate environment. For tennis juniors, parents may not be able to play the direct role that they always want to play on the court – but they *must* do everything in their power to foster a positive, educational, nurturing environment that leads to *real* growth. ***Only*** playing tennis should never be the all-encompassing goal. At least, it shouldn't come from you first. Never! Instead, improvement as a tennis player should arise as a side effect of all the good that the environment is doing for the child.

So, what can parents do to establish the right environments for budding tennis talents? The idea of habit building is central to athlete management. As Will Durant said in 1926, "We are what we repeatedly do. Excellence, therefore, is not an act but a habit."

There will always be variables outside our control, especially in such an unpredictable environment like tennis. However, through persistent effort, we should be able to control the bulk of the variables that impact each athlete's development.

Then comes support, with lots and lots of patience. Remember that results may not show up immediately. This is an over-arching step, though, and it will require ongoing effort. Another point I would make is that parents should realize that seemingly small mistakes (and, likewise, seemingly small improvements) can lead to incredible shifts, for better or for worse.

Long-term thinking: This is what I would like all parents to adopt as a mantra. I find it aggravating to hear parents agree with me verbally and then do nothing to follow through on it. I get that building habits is tough, especially when it's a 24/7 process. Inconsistency, though, will wear away at even the best training program. Because of how big of an issue this can become, I am going to be blunt about it: If you do not respect the rules and if you don't show consistency in your mindsets, standards, goals, and actions, then you should not expect your kid to respect the rules or show consistency, either.

If you expect your kid and coach to be professionals, you have to act like a professional as well. Here is one example: If you know that your behavior at tournaments is going to negatively impact your kid, and you "can't help it," then be professional and don't go. That is what filling your role well as a tennis parent means.

These habits are not meant to lead to results tomorrow, next week, or even next month. We establish these habits so that we can see changes over long stretches of time. Nurturing a passion for self-improvement in general is much more valuable than any specific tennis skill that I could ever teach – and much, much more valuable than any win or loss in competition. Winning and success for a kid should be defined as progressively, gradually, and consistently improving himself or herself both off and on the court, despite adversities. Only through this paradigm can a child develop passion.

Here is a chart that should help you understand the way all the pieces fit together in athlete management. It combines all of the habits that kids need to build and all of the variables that parents need to consider in creating an environment conducive to growth and development.

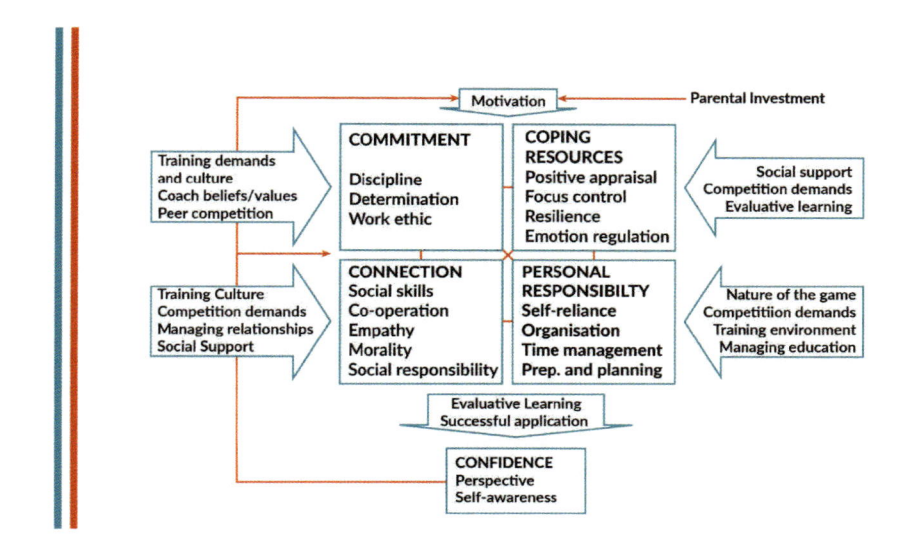

Figure 14. Bronfenbrenner's Environment Systems model adapted for a tennis player

That's why I think using the term "athlete management" here is suitable, because before your kid has a sponsorship deal or a manager in the true sense of the word, you will have to fill that role – from driving them around to practice and tournaments, to hiring the right coaching staff, to making sure they eat the right food and respect curfew hours.

X. Tournaments and Ranking Systems

In all likelihood, you already know a little about tennis tournaments. At the very least, you know what a tennis tournament *is*, so there is no reason for us to start from the definition like we did when we were talking about sports periodization and strategic planning. I will say this, though: Learning more about tennis tournaments will prove advantageous. The more familiar with you are with the rules and regulations from one tournament to the next, from one federation to the next, and from one country to the next, the fewer surprises you are going to encounter.

Say you are trying to plan for the season. You are asking yourself a range of questions. How many tournaments should your kid play in? How do you sign up your kid for a tournament? How does the ranking system work? I will be there to help guide you, but unless you hire a personal coach for your kid from the beginning, you will be driving your young tennis player to and from the tournaments.

Here is where to begin. In every country, the Tennis Federation will provide you with tournament information regarding rules and regulations. Study this information as if there were going to be a test. On www.tennisrecruiting.net, you will find details about college recruiting and the ranking systems that coaches use to identify young talents.

Before you start doing any reading, though, take the time to memorize these abbreviations so that you can talk about all this with other people who are involved in tennis.

UTR – Universal Tennis Rating. This is the newest global tennis player rating system engineered for objectivity, consistency, and accuracy. It looks at players' skills and rates each player on a single 16-point scale without regard to age, gender, nationality, or location.

ITF – International Tennis Federation. This is the governing body of world tennis.

ATP – Association of Tennis Professionals. This is the main governing body of men's professional tennis.

WTA – Women's Tennis Association. This is the main governing body of women's professional tennis.

IPIN – International Player Identification Number. This is a requirement for all players on the ITF Junior and Pro Circuits for simple unique identification.

Here is why you **must** know all of this information: It will lead to better management on your part. Do you need to become a "tournament specialist" and decide, on your own, which tournaments to play? Absolutely not. It will, however, definitely make your life a lot easier.

XI. Positive Player-Parent-Coach Interactions

Here is a list of suggestions; think of them as rules.

Support
- Be patient and allow the child to be in the appropriate stage of development so that he or she can gain confidence and better enjoy playing the game.
- It is best to not watch every match that the child plays, as this can place pressure on him or her.
- Avoid becoming overbearing in your support for your child by keeping lectures about the technicality of tennis to a minimum.
- Stick to your role as the parent; do not try to *become* the coach.
- Playing matches is an important part of a player's development. The child should feel encouraged by the parent to compete as well as have lessons.
- Be aware of the child's capabilities and avoid comparing the child to other players and their development.
- Provide **unconditional** love and support to your child – **WIN or LOSE, tennis or no tennis!** Show emotional neutrality regarding the outcome of a match. Work on it. I know it's easier said than done but you have to train your emotional control. This is as important as your kid learning

how to serve correctly. It's a process for everyone on the team, *not just the kid*.
- Remember to always be a parent first by fostering a positive environment for your child – one that cultivates growth as a ***person before a tennis player***.
- Never assume that you are going to get a "return on your investment." Think of this as something you are doing for your child.

Encourage
- Keep your child accountable for behavior on and off the court. That's not related to the technicals of tennis. Telling your kid to hit more spin on the backhand is *not* it.
- Encourage the child to learn independence. Avoid making him or her too dependent on you.
- Encourage hard work and preparation.
- Focus on effort instead of results. Never ask "Did you win?" Instead, it is better to ask "How did you play?" or "Did you have fun?" Make the child realize that you are more interested in him or her than in the result.

Respect
- Help the child understand that showing respect for the rules, opponents, and officials is all part of tennis.
- Respect the opponents, their parents and coaches, and, of course, the competition officials.
- Always applaud both players.
- The child's coach has the expertise. Respect and appreciate him or her.

Communication
- Clearly communicate expectations with your coach from the beginning.
- Define responsibilities and roles for you and your child's training team from the beginning. Then stick to them!
- Voice concerns with the coach in a way such that the child neither sees nor hears them.

- Periodically schedule quick and simple meetings with your child's coach for progress updates and feedback. Being overbearing, showing up to every practice, and standing on the tennis court with the coach all the time are bad habits, but so are being blasé, knowing nothing, and remaining uninvolved. Focus on trust, honesty, and respect in those meetings. Keep it simple and to the point.

Conclusion

As I am writing this book and thinking about all these topics, it's 2020 and we are in the midst of the global COVID-19 pandemic. My thoughts about this issue are the same as the thoughts that I have presented in this book: Instead of addressing the underlying concerns, we are thinking too much in reaction. Social distancing and wearing face masks may seem to act as preventive measures, but I personally see them as reactive measures. To put this into perspective, why is *no one* talking about how to build better immune systems through proper nutrition, cold water therapy, and sauna?

This is why I recommend adopting systems thinking. Fundamentals before everything else. This is a principle that I am always trying to teach my players, and parents, and it's one more reason why tennis can be so purposeful – not because of the tennis itself but because of what it represents. (Why tennis, right?)

That is why, when I see a kid who is struggling, I must always look at the underlying causes before I can tell them what is wrong with their footwork. It is not always easy to find these problems. However, after all of the years that I have spent in tennis, I have developed an acute sense for them. I have been on every side of this equation. I've made mistakes of my own in the past, and I am trying my best to learn from them. I want to learn as much as I can because I want for myself what I'm advocating for the kids: to pursue mastery through a mental framework of love for knowledge, curiosity, and inspiration. Our main mission, as parents, teachers, coaches, and educators, is to focus on how to achieve that mental framework for our next generation. We have to teach them *how* to think instead of *what* to think if we wish for them to achieve excellence and fulfillment in their professional and personal lives.

As for tennis, there is one thing that will separate an *excellent* training experience from all the rest: a well-functioning training team, with each member recognizing and respecting his or her role and responsibilities. As an expert in your own career, you know the deference you expect regarding your skills and insights. In tennis, the same principles apply, and each member of the team should afford courtesy to coaches and trainers according to their knowledge, understanding, and experience.

Fitness, nutrition, coaching, our habits on the court, our habits off the court: every variable matters. There is no such thing as an "off day" in tennis; there are rest days, definitely, but even those are key to this process. By adhering to this mentality and being patient, the best outcome is within reach.

Having said all that, a child who follows all the right steps in the system may still not become a world-ranked number-one. This is not what I intend this book to accomplish. However, the child will have developed the process mindset and emotional intelligence necessary to cope with adversities in all facets of life and to live a happy life as a well-adjusted adult. Whatever the child wants to do, he or she can do it with confidence. And that's winning in my book.

I hope that you have found some serious value in my book. At the very least, I hope that you are questioning some of the common traps I have seen over the years. One of the most frustrating things that I see for parents is when they come back to me years later only to say "I wish I knew earlier, but it's too late." My quest is to prevent that. I want to educate parents about this sport as much as I can so that their kids can benefit from it in time.

So, *why tennis*? As you realized by now, it's more of a philosophical question. It's about so much more than just tennis, as if your motivations and intentions are imperfect, if your approach is flawed, if you are ignoring blind spots, as I have mentioned, then tennis can become a traumatic experience for your kid. On the flip side, tennis can be a *wonderful* thing. Tennis can nurture positive traits in kids, inspiring them to become the best versions of themselves, no matter what adversities they face, or what the immediate outcome is. I would not have devoted my life to this sport otherwise, right? That is why I think the question "Why tennis?" is both rhetorical in what it implies, and practical, meaning that you need to ask yourself this question first, and you need to answer it honestly. *Why tennis for your kid?*

I will leave you with this quote:

"It is easier to build strong children than to repair broken adults."

~ Frederick Douglass

REFERENCES

January 2015. "Long-Term Athlete Development for the Sport of Tennis in Canada." Tennis Canada.
https://www.tenniscanada.com/wp-content/uploads/2015/01/LTADallenglish.pdf

Dudley, Katherine. 2019 September 24. "Weekend catch-up sleep won't fix the effects of sleep deprivation on your waistline." Harvard Health Publishing.
https://www.health.harvard.edu/blog/weekend-catch-up-sleep-wont-fix-the-effects-of-sleep-deprivation-on-your-waistline-2019092417861

Newman, Paul. 19 August 2016. "Revealed: The diet that saved Novak Djokovic." Independent.
https://www.independent.co.uk/sport/tennis/revealed-the-diet-that-saved-novak-djokovic-8775333.html

Bergeron, M. 30 June 2015. "Hydration in the Pediatric Athlete - How to Guide Your Patients."
Europe PMC. https://europepmc.org/article/med/26166053

Krüger, Arnd. 1973. "Periodization or Peaking at the right time, in: Track Technique." 1720- 1724.

Sportlyzer. https://academy.sportlyzer.com/wiki/arousal-and-performance/individual-zones-of-optimal-functioning-izof/

Csikszentmihalyi, Mihaly. 2014. "Flow and the Foundations of Positive Psychology."

Ford, P.; De Ste Croix, M.; Lloyd, R.; Meyers, R.; Moosavi, M.; Oliver, J.; Till, K.; Williams, C.
    2011 February. "The Long-Term Athlete Development Model: Physiological Evidence and Application." National Library of Medicine. https://pubmed.ncbi.nlm.nih.gov/21259156/

Durant, Will. 1926. *The Story of Philosophy: The Lives and Opinions of the World's Greatest Philosophers.*

Matt Kuzdub 2019 *"Beyond the swing"*

Printed in Great Britain
by Amazon